D1826119

# An Imaginary Affair

## Poems Whispered to Neruda

*poems by*

# Diana Raab

*Finishing Line Press*
Georgetown, Kentucky

# An Imaginary Affair

## Poems Whispered to Neruda

## ACKNOWLEDGMENTS

Grateful acknowledgements to the following literary journals where some of
the poems in this chapbook have been published:

"Lonely Death;" "Haunted Beginnings" (as "Beginnings") *RavensPerch*
"Please Be Still" (as "Stillness"); "The Unfolding" *The Mindful Word*
"Ode to Memory" *Book of Odes; Poets' Choice*
"Tonight I Can Write" *Sunspot Literary*
"Shadows of Our Past" (as "Shadows") *Black Coffee Review*
"My Heart Broke Loose With the Wind" *Spillway*
"I Love Your Sonnet" *Capsule Stories*
"Craving You;" "My Desire for You" (as "Desire") *Last Leaves Magazine*
"My Heart Broke Loose With the Wind;" "Your Smile" (as "His Smile")
        *While You Wait: Anthology*. Gunpowder Press

Publisher: Leah Huete de Maines
Editor: Christen Kincaid
Cover Art: Shutterstock / Contributor: puhhha
Author Photo: Mark Singer
Cover Design: Andrew Bell

Order online: www.finishinglinepress.com
        also available on amazon.com

Author inquiries and mail orders:
Finishing Line Press
PO Box 1626
Georgetown, Kentucky 40324
USA

# Table of Contents

*For*
*Pablo Neruda*
*(1904 - 1973)*

*"You can cut all the flowers but you cannot keep*
*the spring from coming."*
*~ Pablo Neruda*

# DEDICATION

We all stand on the shoulders of giants. Poet Pablo Neruda is my primary giant for this chapbook, but it would never have been actualized without the professional and emotional support of a number of individuals in my personal life. It's impossible to mention everybody who has touched me over the past six decades, so please forgive me if your name is not mentioned here. You know who you are.

In particular, there are a few friends and colleagues who need special acknowledgment, as they were consistently present—and inspiring—on my literary path. It all began with my sixth-grade English teacher in Queens, New York, who was from Chile, and whose compliments gave me the courage to become a poet and a writer. Since then, there have been so many others who have touched my creative spirit. More recently, I'd like to acknowledge the following individuals for encouraging the poet in me: Kim Stafford, Tristine Rainer, Perie Longo, David Starkey, Chryss Yost, George Yatchisin, Susan Wooldridge, Jill Kramer, Marilyn Kapp, Alexis Rhone Fancher, Jon Hess, and especially Laure-Anne Bosselaur, who graciously and enthusiastically helped me bring this project to fruition. Also, I'd like to thank Dr. Tim Frank and Pam Lancaster for their intuitive wisdom and friendship over the years.

Most importantly, I want to thank my beloved husband Simon, who has been my guiding light, and whose love and support has been behind every one of my creative endeavors. Also, I send deep gratitude to my loving and creative children and their partners: Rachel Raab, Richard Bassett, Regine Raab del Valle, Daniel del Valle, Joshua Samuel Raab, Marley Chamoi Raab; and my grandchildren: Jaxson Alexander Bassett, Lilly Rachel Bassett, Lila Mae del Valle, Nico Ernesto Edward del Valle, and Jahji Siddhartha, for always surrounding me with love.

And, of course, huge gratitude to Pablo Neruda (born Ricardo

Elicer Neftali Reyes) for his exuberant, sensual, passionate, and intimate poetry, which has inspired me and so many others. His poetry clearly transcends the ordinary and transforms readers over and over again.

## The Unfolding

Peeling an apple in one piece,
I think of our friendship unfolding.

At the café, our eyes married right there.
Such impatient anticipation.

Was this desire one-sided?
I was curious about so much—

would you fulfill my fantasies,
or walk away indifferent to my gaze?

The second time revealed more.
I studied your approach—

what you wore, what you said.
Then your decision: where to plant

that first kiss, hunting for the best
private spot until our next encounter.

For you would return, after all.

## My Heart Broke Loose With the Wind

On the pages of a Khalil Gibran journal
my voice was freed—the wind squalled
through my brain beaten
down by words, abusive.

Such liberation possessed me wholly.
His revelation bloomed,
so unlike my mother's mutterings
as she drifted in and out of madness.

My lines, at ten, engendered
many other poems holding and healing
me—once so deeply shattered.
Those words now yearning for the divine
just like the prophet Khalil Gibran.

## Ode to Memory

From the moment I rise in the morning
how I remember everything
where my slippers sleep,
how to get downstairs,
where to find my dog
and how to brew my coffee.

I love to remember
my first coffee in a Parisian café
at age sixteen with grandpa—
strong espresso and sugar cube,
and how the server was so kind.

I will always remember
not what people do for me,
nor what they say,
but how they make me feel.

I will always remember my first love,
how and where it happened,
the sound of his name,
and how he held me,

and how scared
we were when blood gushed from me
onto his parent's bed,
them at movie theater,
and how embarrassed I was,
yet how close it made us.

I'll always remember
the feeling of being loved
in that way—for the very first time.

## Honoring Our Past

Like the past we walked, my beloved.
We cannot recover nor paint again
our stories, streets and avenues occupied
by this past and aware that we are
all going home after another day of blues.

Tangled in one another,
let's rejoice on this one day
in this life's flash, and remember
there's no turning back.

## Getting Lost Together

I am in the forest where you had been lost, and found
the tree where you pressed my hand to your heart.

I am peaceful now. Grateful for this solitary moment.
And thank my ancestors for ushering me along the way

to you. How we can now let go of so much,
and allow one another in.

## Haunted Beginnings

You speak of your troubled beginnings
as if your life was forged, shaped by them
into your quotidian.

I don't see that in your mirror—
nor do I find in the poems you wrote
out of this trauma.

Dear one,
you are no different from any other poet
before or after you whose past

drove them to these shared pages—
like me, etching my words,
locked in my childhood closet,

haunted by the mystery
of my grandmother's suicide—
and those bottles, those many bottles of pills
bringing her to die in my arms.

How could this not leave
a scorching in me
who hears and shares the intimacy
of the poet you have become?

## I Love Your Sonnet

Dear Pablo:

Loving you is as easy as my breath
in and out, which sustains me
when we're apart. You might think
you don't know me—but I am the magic
that reaches for you in the night's gloom,
and the shooting star that blasts
its way to your garden's horizon.
Can you feel my gentle hand upon
your shoulder: a hummingbird's
happy flutter? Come lay your head
on my feathery pillow.
Leave your garden for mine.
I have been waiting long enough.
This is my sonnet for you.

## Kisses and Rhetoric

When we lie together,
me on your closely shaven chest

your legs snaked about mine,
there's a pile of smudged tongue kisses

all around us. One can get lost
in this sense of euphoria,

this after-sex delight
when everything seems right

within our boundaries —
until I turn to you

in that ten minute window
asking for your thoughts.

You smile, kiss my forehead
and squeeze my arm:

that's a rhetorical question, you say.
And return again to your kisses

as your heart beats into mine
and time slithers ever so slowly

around our temporary universe.

**Craving You**

This morning, you stand at your shower door—
peek as you enter under water droplets,
I peer through frosted glass and yearn

for you to hold me, lift me up
and twirl me around, like the ballerina
we loved at last night's show.

I want to do everything with you:
watch you place two steaks
on our barbeque, baste potatoes,

and lick ice cream drips from your cone,
and sprinkle me with kisses. I want
no sunrises and sunsets without you,

but long for fleeting rainbows to encircle us
and shooting stars, the guards of all our wishes.

## My Desire for You

I lust after every part of you—every one. Your mouth—that lake
where we met—and your eyes, brilliant as its waters.

We walked slowly on that lake's edge, afraid to leap in too fast,
afraid to dip into dangers in its depths.

You kissed every fingerbreadth of my body. Even my scars
enchanted you—oh, and how another human could be formed

with those stitches that hold me together.
Was there one part of my body you didn't cherish?

Your tongue slithered— a tiny snake—up and down my aging body.
It sang under that spell. You loved my years, a twinkle in each
wrinkle.

Your cerulean gaze lit my crevices
all at once limp and tense
with desire. I watched you mirror my lust.

Such tantric waiting! We waited and waited until I could no longer
keep my hands and mouth away from you.

And I remembered: just allow, be with it—once again
we were brought to desire's edge, before reality grabbed us back.

## Your Smile

Take my diamonds, bury my treasures
and burn my books, but never
take away your smile.

Don't take back the carnation you picked
as a child, the baby food left on porcelain plates
or that golden light on everything
on the day you were born, son.

Your sadness—each day of it—
pools into the lining of me: those many worlds
on your brow and in your gaze's shadow.

Let me tug them from you as you sleep
not far from the turbulent ocean:
such mystery and regret.

I smile at you.
You didn't smile back then.
But you do, now.
I walk away, glowing.

## Why Are You Sad?

Dear Pablo:

Why are you so very sad?

As you cast your gaze
in my direction, those blue
puddles color thoughts from beyond:
from what pasts, what diaspora?

Come back to me—bear witness
to who I am, who I will be with you,
bear witness as the morning
pulls us toward noon.

Without you, I wear only darkness.
That's what fate bestowed on me:
annihilation in my history.

The sky shivers—noon gallops
into a new night over a horizon ,
waiting for your sadness to squander.

## Ode to Hot Toddy on a Sick Day

Golden-colored hot toddy, you glisten
under tonight's moon sliver
as my throat aches for you.
Your golden light flashes your love,
flecks of lemon rind float about this whiskey
swirled with honey from the bee that loves
that buzz you give me.

Never has one night been enough with you, Toddy,
sipping from your cup, Toddy:
my soothing drink, glittered
with your love—tangy
with the healing powers of ginger—
silky like my legs cozy
in the blankets,
such longing brings me to you, Toddy.

I can drink you over and over again
to welcome in or end my day
as I ebb from sickness to health
with your sweetness, amorous,
glistening.
Your hues brighten my night,
my delicious love.
But more than sipping you,
it's your colors
that sing the flames in my fever:
an abundant and floral fragrance
of you and your tipsy
presence in my life.

## Please Be Still

I like for you to be still—
but only if you can be

still beside me
under a palm tree

beneath my rainbow
inside my marrow

which craves the rhythms
of your enfolding body.

Today I look into your eyes
they are dry—

no glisten like yesterday
nor whisper of loneliness—

just neutral, as you breathe out
melancholy and inhale bliss.

I speak to your silence
and crave to have you inside me.

Present. Still. Enough.

## Our Invisible Love

When we stroll down city streets
during our lives' twilight
passersby have no idea

who we are or where we're going.
You come into my world,
one moment at a time to listen

to my confidences with your ear-
bending heart, and I enter into
your lonely life as I listen to you.

Then, suddenly, you're gone,
but know that you're all I want right now,
as I recede alone into my evenings

yearning to share with you, looking
down on those city streets
as stars shimmer above, only for us.

## The Shadows of Our Past

As we enter our last decades
shouldn't we look back at
the shadows that both lurk in our past
and follow us?

Where will you find me
if not under your patch of love
that blossoms with the rain
and opens one petal at a time—

away from this hurt hammered
into the seed of me. I dare you
take anything from me or
I shall be gone.

## Listen to Me

Listen to me
when I speak to you.
Listen to me tell you
that I will never leave
what we call us.

What I fear most
is that you'll leave me
in the cold of a night
when I least expect or want it
because ennui
meandered through you,

and I fear: will you run from me
when trains sleep at their stations,
dogs bark at coyotes,
and owls share their wisdom?

## A Final Refuge

You remember my voice
even though I have

long ago peeled myself
from you, your shoulder,

on that crisp autumn day
as the pungent smell

of burning leaves
fell from our sky.

Your voice still resonates
even though

I am in that other world,
because this one

has transitioned,
it no longer serves

nor wants to witness us—
a love that's so deep.

Will you accompany me
to this final refuge?

## Mourning Lament

Such death within our heart's chambers:
the beloved lamenting under the temples'
arches, coming alive again as we call to them,
desperate to make sense of their death.

And we move together slowly, one step
at a time toward another dance, another life,
in which we would return and find solace
in the warm chambers that sustain us.

## Waving Goodbye to Life

There are times when I'm also tired
of this journey we call life.

You see, I've done all that needs
to be done, welcomed many moons,

climbed many mountains, nurtured
children from my aging womb,

welcomed grandchildren, cherished
loyal dogs, battled cancer, taught

many to write, cared for a volatile mother.
I've paid my dues. I paid them all.

I am ready to wave goodbye to memories
and bow to gratitude—

offer a love, profound now, and take in
the passion which has sustained us.

And so it is. Please let me
go now...please.

## Lonely Death

There are people who die
surrounded by loved ones
and others die alone
to shiver in their own fearful inquiry.

Standing here
at the cusp of a rolling hill cemetery,
survivors and I come together
to write to our beloveds,

all I can visualize
are pine boxes of shriveled humans
lined up in rows—
no longer submitting to rules or rage.

All that's important is
that your beloved places
stones upon your grave
or that a ghost sometimes
appears in your nights
whispering a blessing.

How long does it take
for a pine casket to disintegrate
in this caving land—
not forgotten, so alone?

I've always been drawn to death—
mine perished in the Holocaust—
a persistent life theme
unable to bury
as long as my feet
touch the ardent earth.

## Tonight I Can Write

I thought he would be with me
until our end. I had to say goodbye
to him who rests, now, six feet above,
six feet below a night we only knew.

I wanted to be who he awakened to
each morning, not who he waved
goodbye to across our ocean
or those stars which lit only
our shadows.

He named me to her, his wife:
she tied his hands, in prayer
behind his back, resigned, exhausted
to what was to be his fate.

I am left orphaned by a love
which promised to give—
shattered now—rich only with
imagined memories, the oceans
and its stars my only light.

## Please Don't Forget Me

I want you to know
one thing:

if there is ever a day
when you begin to think
about my place in this world
and if I could live without you—

stop in your tracks,
and look at the imprints
your feet made in the sand
where you and I walked together
arm in arm, side by side
shoulder touching shoulder.

You are ingrained in my brain
like every kernel of sand
that lies beside the largest ocean
in this world where we inhabit
two sides familiar, yet foreign
to one another.  But, in the end,

I had to let you go: when you love
someone it's what one must do —
set them free to do what they need
or want, and when they want

to do it, whether it is with you or not—
while always keeping in mind
I will never in my lifetime or yours
stop loving everything about you.

# Notes

"The Unfolding," in response to 'XVII I do not love you,'
    by Pablo Neruda

"My Heart Broke Loose With the Wind," in response to 'Poetry'
    by Pablo Neruda

"I Love Your Sonnet," in response to 'Sonnet XVII' by Pablo Neruda

"Invisible Love," in response to 'Clenched Souls' by Pablo Neruda

"Please Be Still," in response to 'I Like for You To Be Still'
    by Pablo Neruda

"Craving You," in response to 'I Crave Your Mouth, Your Voice,
    Your Hair' by Pablo Neruda

"My Desire for You," in response to: 'Love Sonnet XI'
    by Pablo Neruda

"Getting Lost Together," in response to 'Lost in the Forest'
    by Pablo Neruda

"Ode to Hot Toddy on a Sick Day," in response to 'Ode to Wine'
    by Pablo Neruda

"Please Don't Forget Me," in response to 'If You Forget Me,'
    by Pablo Neruda

"Listen to Me," in response to 'Don't Go Far Off,' by Pablo Neruda

"Ode to Memory," in response to 'Memory' by Pablo Neruda

"Your Smile," in response to 'Your Laughter' by Pablo Neruda

"Honoring Our Past," in response to 'Past' by Pablo Neruda

"Kisses and Rhetoric," in response to 'Drunk as Drunk'
    by Pablo Neruda

"Tonight I Can Write," in response to 'Tonight I Can Write the
    Saddest Lines' by Pablo Neruda

"A Final Refuge," in response to 'Your Voice Peels' by Pablo Neruda

"Shadows of Our Past," in response to 'It Means Shadows'
    by Pablo Neruda

"Mourning Lament," in response to 'Ode to Lament'
    by Pablo Neruda

"Waving Goodbye to Life," in response to 'Walking Around'
    by Pablo Neruda

"Lonely Death," in response to 'Nothing But Death' by Pablo Neruda

Diana Raab, MFA, PhD, is a poet, memoirist, and blogger, and the award-winning author of nine books. Her work has been published and anthologized in more than 1,000 publications. Raab has four poetry collections: *Dear Anais: My Life in Poems for You*, *The Guilt Gene*, *Listening to Africa*, and *Lust*. Raab has written another chapbook, *My Muse Undresses Me*. She blogs for *Psychology Today*, *Thrive Global*, and *The Wisdom Daily*, and is a guest blogger for many other publications and websites. Her latest nonfiction books are *Writing for Bliss: A Seven-Step Program for Telling Your Story and Transforming Your Life* and *Writing for Bliss: A Companion Journal*. One of her recent creative endeavors is Conversation Cards for Meaningful Storytelling, which can also be used as poetry prompts. She frequently speaks and writes about the healing and transformative powers of writing prose and poetry. Visit her at: dianaraab.com.

CPSIA information can be obtained
at www.ICGtesting.com
Printed in the USA
JSHW061140090722
27779JS00003B/235

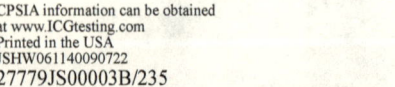

9 781646 628315